THE
SWORD
OF
PROST

AN ADVENTURE
IN WHICH YOU ARE THE HERO

Dedication

*To the two Jamies,
Brother and son.
One for Inspiration,
The other for fun.*

Learning Development Aids
Duke Street
Wisbech
Cambs PE13 2AE
England

The Sword of Prost   Ref no. LD783

© Living & Learning (Cambridge) Ltd 1987

First printed 1987
Reprinted 1987, 1990, 1991

ISBN 0-905114-25-6

THE SWORD OF PROST

by
Dr Michael Thomson

with illustrations
by Tim Oliver

LDA

Learning Development Aids

Note for teachers, parents (and readers)

The reader begins at number one. Thereafter he or she makes decisions which determine which page is read next.

Readers will need:

A copy of the adventure sheet at the back of this book. (This may be freely photocopied.) During their adventure readers will need to fight off many of the creatures they encounter. The adventure sheet helps them to keep a record of their victories and losses.

Two dice. Each time a reader fights a creature they will throw their two dice. The number they throw is entered in the 'Fighting Skills' column alongside the name of the creature. Pupils then add the dice throw to the number already in the column, which gives them a value for their fighting skills.

The story will tell them the fighting skill of the creature. The greater number wins.

A Pencil.

Each time a reader stops reading The Sword of Prost, he or she must note the story number they have got to on their adventure sheet. This will enable them to continue their adventure later.

Teachers may also find that pupils will enjoy writing about what has happened to them so far.

THE SWORD OF PROST
1

You are the Ruler of the Secret Land. You beat the evil Grom to become Ruler. (Read about what happened in The Castle of Grom.) You have also proved to be a fit Ruler and had the power given to you. (Read about what happened in The Crown of the Sun-King.)

Now you must go on a quest to repair the Sword of Prost.

You will need a copy of the adventure sheet at the back of this book, a pencil and two dice.

Look at your adventure sheet. It lists all the creatures you may have to fight. You may not meet all these creatures and you may not meet them in this order. Each time you fight a creature remember to fill in your adventure sheet. The story will tell you how.

Sometimes you can choose to fight using Weapons, Combat or Magic. Choose wisely. Think about the creature you are fighting. Try to choose something he is not good at. The story will help.

Your adventure sheet shows you that you have 25 Life points. You may lose Life points in your adventure. You may also be given some more. Be careful, if you lose all your Life points you die!

Your adventure sheet shows you that you have an Equipment List. You will be given many useful things on your journey. Remember to write them on your Equipment List. They may help you mend the Sword of Prost.

If you have read the Castle of Grom and The Crown of the Sun King you will have useful equipment that you may use here. If you have the **Crown** and the **broken bits of the Sword of Prost** write them onto the Sword of Prost Equipment List.

Your adventure sheet also shows you that you have a list of Questers. To mend the Sword of Prost you must find helpers from each of the main races. They will join you on your quest. Each time someone joins you on your quest you must write their name down on the list of Questers.

Finally, remember to write down the number you are on when you finish reading. Do this in the 'story number' column on your adventure sheet.

It is a shame that your new rule is not going too well. You are Ruler over many kinds of people. They seem to fight all the time. You are always having to stop these fights. Now it seems that the Dragons are to fight with the Men of the Plains. The Elves are about to start a war with the Dwarves. This would be bad on its own, but there is more. There is a kingdom near the Secret Land. It is called Morash. The King of Morash is Salim. The Kingdom of Morash has some magic of its own.

Salim is always trying to take over the Secret Land. This takes the form of a Challenge every year. The ruler of the Secret Land must beat Salim. In the past the ruler has always won. The Challenge is next month. The Sword of Prost, your magic sword, is broken. (Read about what happened in The Crown of the Sun-King.) You are not at all sure that you can win without it.

As you think on all this a visitor arrives. You look up and see a woman dressed in a blue robe. She must have come in while you were thinking. She has sea-green eyes and looks into your eyes. She raises her hands and you feel her mind in yours. Will you let her into your mind — 47 or try a spell to cast her out — 111.

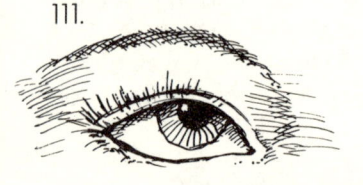

2

You thrust your sword between the Worm's scales. Thin, green blood comes out. The worm does not seem to notice. Its vast mouth opens up. You see the teeth that grind the jewels. You thrust your sword into the soft back of the Worm's throat. The Worm rises up into the air. You hear a high scream. The Worm turns and goes out of the tunnel. It is never seen again. You have won! Add one to your Life point score.

Thon is very pleased. He gives you a large, blue jewel. It is the **Gem of Wisdom.** Write it down on your equipment list. The Dwarf King also sends his son, Ganli, to help you on your Quest. Write **Ganli** on your list of Questers. Do you have all 5 Questers now? If you have Mork the Dragon, Rula the Woman, Hamid the Elf, Lori the Magi and Ganli the Dwarf — 165. If not — 81 and choose where to go next.

3

You cannot make the new Sword without the mould. You will have to go back to the old elf city and visit the Docks — 56.

4

You draw your sword. The yellow shape gets close. It opens it's mouth — 106.

5

The Crown glows brightly. It gets hot and you do not feel any cold left in your body. The Elf does not smile now! In fact he does not look at all happy. He begins to fade away. Just before he goes he looks at one of the shelves. There is a book on the shelf. You go over and open the book. Inside is a folded bit of paper. You take it out and unfold it. It is a map! Clearly marked is Death Mountain and the Elf Forge! This is a great bit of luck. Add one to your Life point score. Write down the **map** on your Equipment List.

You can now go to the Docks — 56, go and find the others by the Gate — 36, or visit the underground Caves — 119.

6

Slowly you begin to catch up. The Elf's breath is coming in gasps now. You see the finish line ahead. You hear the roar of the crowd. The Elf is a few metres from the line. You fling yourself at the line! You win by a nose!

The Elf Queen is surprised by your running — 82.

7

You try to cast a spell. The Water Beast looks at you again. Its eyes glow. You feel very sleepy and cannot move. You try to say your spell. The Water Beast has great Magic power. You will have a hard fight.

The **Water Beast** has 16 Fighting Skill points.

If you win — 33, if you lose — 118.

8

One by one you enter the mine. You go round a corner. There is a cave here. Just as you are all in, Trolls jump up from rocks all around you. It is a trap! But how did the Trolls know that you would come this way? You have no more time to think about this as the Trolls attack. You see the others fighting. Mork flames two Trolls down, and Rula holds three at bay. Ganli hits out with his axe. Lori's magic darts blue fire around and Hamid's arrows fly into Trolls' chests. There are still too many!

Then you see a huge Troll. He is 8 metres tall with strong, hairy limbs. He roars at you. You see sharp teeth in his great mouth. He has thick claws on hands and feet. This is the **Troll King.** Prepare for battle. Throw your dice and work out your Fighting Skill. The Troll King has a sword which glows a little. Some of the magic of the ore must have got into his sword. That will have to be taken care of too! Will you use Combat — 128, Magic — 48 or Weapons — 87?

9

Mork agrees to fly you to the Castle. The rest of your Questers go to their homes. Lori says that the Magi will not forget what you have done. The others all promise true friendship.

You fly on with Mork. You fly high and fast over hill and dale. After the first day you have gone over half of the way to the Castle. You are making good time — 14.

10

Rula can do nothing. She cannot reach up that far and has no Magic — 142.

11

You try to cast a spell. The Demon seems to shake in the air. It cannot be seen for a little while. Then it is back in the air. You try all your Magic powers. At last you use up all your Magic for the moment. The Demon still stares at you. You can use Weapons — 141, Combat — 32, or ask the others to help — 151.

12

You look at Ganli. He gives you a wink. He marches over to Lori. He looks very stern. He looks Lori in the eyes. Ganli then, very slowly, takes out his axe. You see that his eyes seem to be getting red. Ganli raises the axe above his head. Lori looks scared. He knows what Dwarves are like when they go battle mad. Lori thinks that his life is about to end. He agrees to help! The only problem now is what to do! — 66.

13

You go to see the Dragons. You go across the land that has been laid waste by the Dragons' fire. At last you come to the Dragon caves. There you meet the Golden Dragon. He is the King of the Dragons. He wears the circle of the Dragon King. You tell him of your Quest. He tells you of a huge Black Dragon that has been killing other Dragons. He is evil and mad. He is also very strong. He asks your help. If you will fight the Black Dragon — 139, if you will not help — 81.

14

It is now Day 2 of your trip back to the castle. You get on to Mork's back. You think that you will have a lot of time to get ready for Salim. Then the air gets dark. It feels cold and clouds form high and deep. A storm is coming. Mork starts to fly down to the lands. He cannot fly in a storm. Then you feel the slash of lightening. A crack of thunder! You feel yourself falling. Mork is blown away. The wind is too strong! You crash to the ground! — 19.

15

You are wrong in thinking that this will be easy! The Magi let you win when you were in their city. Magi are the best Magic users in the land. You have not got the full power of the Mace, Crown and the Sword. Lose 2 Life points. You must try Weapons — 58, or Combat — 127.

16

You go past the face. You all come to some passages in the rock. You now need to find the Elven Forge. You tell the others to go down the passages to look. You will all meet up later. You go on alone. After a while you see a light up ahead. It is the end of the passage. You come out into an old crater. The mountain was once a volcano. The passage comes out into the floor of the crater. It is now covered in sand. A high wall of rock is all round. It is like a vast arena. Around the arena, in the dark rock wall, are openings. These are where other passages go into the arena. In the middle of the arena is a large stone. It has a flat top. You walk over to the stone. There you see a map. It has been carved into the stone. The map is the same as the one that you got from the Dark Elf. It also shows the part that was taken from the other map. You shout "I've found it! I've found it!"

Then, from all around, come the rest of the Questers. One comes from each of the openings in the rock wall around the arena. There is Mork, the Dragon, with her wings up and ready to flame. Hamid, the Elf, has his bow up with an arrow ready to shoot. You see Lori, the Magi, with his hands in the air and a spell on his lips. In yet another opening is Ganli, the Dwarf, his axe held high. Rula, the Woman, has her sword in her hand and looks ready to run. They seem to think you are in danger. They must have heard you shout. You think about the traps and the bit of map going missing. One of them must want very badly to stop the Quest. But who? Which one has been creeping up to kill you? Which one has come to save you? — 17.

17

One of your band has not been for the Quest. Which one is the spy?

> Mork, the Dragon — 155
> Lori, the Magi — 42
> Ganli, the Dwarf — 85
> Rula, the Woman — 126
> Hamid, the Elf — 96

18

You thrust at the bear with your sword. He charges at you. The sword sticks in his leg. The rush of the bear pulls the sword from your hands. The sword still sticks in the bear. It is hurt and this makes it wild with pain! Try Combat — 136.

19

You wake up after a time. The storm has blown Mork away. You were lucky that you were not hurt. Your fall was on to a grass bank. You rolled down the bank. You look up at the sky. You have been knocked out for a long time. You are now in Day 3. You have come half-way with three days to go. Now you can only go two ways to the Castle, into the Desert — 152 or into the Swamp — 167.

20

You head for the tents where the Magic trials are being held. The people still do not see who you are. Some look at you as if they seem to know you. The first rounds of the Magic trials are simple tricks and childrens' games. At last you meet someone to match your power. In the final you meet a woman with an Orb of Power. It is the Magic Mistress. The woman is tall with violet eyes and a slender figure. You both bow. She casts her hands over the Orb. Violet light springs forth. The light forms ropes to bind you. Battle starts!

The **Magic Mistress** has 21 Fighting Skill points.

If you lose — 34, if you win — 109.

21

The Elven Forge is a pool of red hot lava in the ground. There is a block of stone, like an anvil, near the pool of lava. There is also a pool of water there. It is still and clear blue. You take out the bits of the Sword of Prost. Lori laughs. "You need all the races of the land to help to forge the Sword. I will not help." Mork flames a little. Lori pales but still will not help. Mork looks at you. You know that the dragon will not harm anyone unless in battle. Who will help here? — 147.

22

You take out the Sword of Prost. The Eagle is angry that you will fight it. It attacks. You turn to one side and slice its head off. The Sword has power now! The Eagle lies dead. It is a pity that you no longer have time to get to the Castle. Salim takes over the Kingdom because you are not at the Field of Challenge in time!

23

You strike at the Dragon. Your sword does not hurt him. You strike again and the sword is twisted from you. You take up a combat stance. You leap on to the Black Dragon as he goes past. You try for his weak spot — 24.

24

You twist your hands into the Black Dragon's neck. He gives out a shout of rage and pain. He tries to shake you off. You hang on. At last the nerve hold pays off. The dragon crashes to the ground. You leap off as the Dragon breaks his neck. You look at the Dragon. You are sorry that such a fine thing was evil. Add one point to your Life Point Score. The Dragon King is very pleased. He tells you that he will send one of the Dragons with you on your Quest. It is a Dragon that he trusts. It is one of Bork's family. She is called Mork. Write **Mork** on your list of Questers. You greet Mork and you set off again. How many Questers have you got now? If you have Mork the Dragon, Rula the Woman, Hamid the Elf, Ganli the Dwarf and Lori the Magi — 165. If you do not have all 5 Questers — 81 and choose where to go next.

25

The Dark Elf slashes at you. You duck to one side. You try to thrust home but he crashes his sword onto yours. You twist your sword to one side. Then you get past his guard. You hold the sword to his throat — 38.

26

You ask Hamid to come forward. You hope that the face will see that he is an Elf and let you past. The face says, "Who dares enter the Mount of the Elves?" Hamid answers that he is an Elf and wants to go to the Elven Forge. The face says, "Be he Elf or not, any who go to the Forge must pass me, or fight the Demon". Will you fight the Demon — 83, or check your Equipment List to see if anything will help — 39.

27

He keeps slipping from your grip. At last you twist his arm and throw him. He jumps up and a blow to your stomach has you gasping. Then, using a leg throw, you hurl him out of the ring. The crowd cheers. You are given the prize for the Combat trials. Now you must go for the Magic trials. Prepare to fight the **Magic Mistress.** Throw your dice and work out your Fighting skill — 20.

28

As you went into his cave you think that it is not fair to kill the bear. You chant a spell. "Go to sleep, not a peep!" The bear's eyes get heavy. He gets very sleepy. He falls to the ground. You go out of the cave and hurry up the path — 148.

29

Mork flies up after Lori. Dragon's are very quick in the air and have some Magic power. Mork's magic is able to fend off Lori just for the time it takes to flame at him a little. Lori is not very brave. He comes down to the ground at once. On the way down he throws the bit of the Sword of Prost out over the rock wall. It lands on top of the wall. The rock is sheer. It has few hand holds. Mork guards Lori. You will need to get the Bit of the Sword. You are not a very good climber. Who will help you? — 31.

30

The woman is the same one that told the Sun-King about the Crown. She tells you that the Crown gives power to the Ruler, but all three things are needed. These are the Crown, the Mace and the Sword of Prost. The Sword is needed for the Challenge of Salim and to bring the people to peace. She tells you that there is a way to mend the Sword. You can take it to the Lost Forge of the Elves. You need to find this. You also need the help of all the people of the Land.

The words in your mind fade away. When you look up there is no one there. Was it a dream?

Will you go on a Quest for the Lost Forge of the Elves — 79, or will you fight Salim first — 93.

31

You must choose someone to help you: Rula — 53, Hamid — 159, Ganli — 117.

32

You try and get near the Demon to attack it. You cannot get near. The more you push to get to it, the more the air pushes you back. You can try Magic — 11, Weapons — 141 or ask the others to help — 151.

33

You shake off the sleepy feeling. You look away from its eyes. You say "Beast down, Beast drown!" The Water Beast falls back into the river. It goes down deep and you are safe. You can look at the cases in the corner of the room — 137.

34

You try to start the Magic of the Crown. Too late! The violet ropes have tied you up. You have lost the trials. Some of the people then see who you are. They will not have a Ruler who can be beaten in the trials. Salim has won.

You have failed at the last!

35

You stop and call to the Eagle. At first it does not seem to hear you. Then, at last, its great wings fold up. The Eagle dives down at you. Will it see who you are? Will it care who you are? Is it going to attack? The Eagle's sharp beak slices nearer. Its huge body rushes down. Will you use Weapons — 22, Combat — 50, Magic — 133 or take out the Mace — 104.

36

At the end of the day you head to the Gate. There you meet up with the others on the Quest. None of the others seem to have found anything. You need the **Magic Metal,** The **Map** and the magic word **"Tsorp"** if your Quest is to be successful. (If you have not got all of them you must go to the Library — 84, the Cave — 119 or the

Docks — 56.)

Rula tells you that she saw a figure running away down a dark passage. Mork says that he went down by the river. As he flew over he saw a huge Water Beast. Ganli and Hamid seem to have spent most of the time telling each other where to go! (Dwarves and Elves do not always get on.) Lori says that he looked at some old books, but that none were any help.

You tell the others what you found. Lori asks to look at the magic metal sword shape. You show it to him. You all then make camp for the night. It has been a busy day. You rest and eat a meal. Mork roasts some meat with her breath. Rula sings while Hamid plays a flute he had in his pack. Then Lori shows some Magic tricks. Finally Ganli tells you long stories of Dwarf history. Dwarf stories are always very, very long. You all fall asleep. Still, it has been a great night. Add four Life points to your Life point score — 92.

37

The men go. You wait and wait. Salim does not come. The next day he claims the Kingdom. You did not meet the Challenge!

You have failed at the last!

38

The Dark Elf tries to turn away. You just make a little cut on his skin. He gives up at once. He tells you that he knows of your Quest. He is part of a group of Elves who stayed behind in the city after the others left. Over the years they have become twisted and evil. He has no interest in your Quest, but he wants you to let him go. He tells you that he has a secret that you must know. If you will let him go he will tell you. If you agree go to — 61, if you want to kill him go to — 91.

39

You can use the Crown of the Sun-King — 52, the word of power given by the Dark Elf (Tsorp) — 108, or some of the Magic Ore from Death Mountain — 74.

40

You back off. If you can stay out of reach the dagger and sword are no match for the Sword of Prost. You do not want to hurt your Captain. You feel a little like a cheat as the Sword of Prost lights up with its power. The Captain steps forward. You duck and bring the Sword onto his head, flat side of the blade first. The Captain falls to the ground. He gets up with a grin and a bump on his head. He salutes. The crowd cheers as they see who you are at last. You promise to do your best against Salim. You then go off to find Gamesmaster again — 63.

41

You think about your last fight with a Dragon. That was with Bork, who then became your friend. He told you how Dragons think that they cannot be beaten by a small human. You made a fool of him with your Combat skills. You try the same thing with the Black Dragon. You will take him by surprise.

The Black Dragon sneers as he sees that you have no weapon. He flies by just to show how great he is. He is just going by when you take a leap. You end up on his back. You then turn over and cling to his underside. You try and put a nerve lock onto the weak spot in his neck. Can you do it?

The **Black Dragon** has 9 Fighting Skill points.

If you win — 24, if you lose — 71.

42

You look at Lori. He is small. He could have been the figure you saw in the desert, so could Ganli. Yet Ganli told you about the Trolls. Why would he do that if he was then going to tell them to ambush you? Also that globe must have been Magic. You recall how easy it was for you to beat all the Magi at Magic. They must have wanted Lori to come on the Quest. Yes, it must be Lori! — 134.

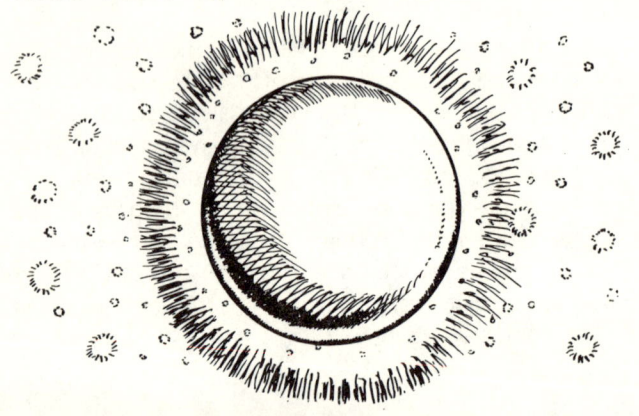

43

The Dark Elf's sword lights up red. He has some Magic too. It is too strong for you! You draw your sword and charge! — 135.

44

You go and look for Salim. He does not seem to be around. You see some tents in the Castle grounds. You see one of Salim's men. You go up to him and ask where Salim is. He looks at you. All at once he grins. "Come this way, Oh Ruler". He takes you into a tent. Here five armed men grab you. They gag you and tie you up. You are dumped in the corner of the tent. Salim has told his men to look out for you. He knew you were away. He hoped to capture you so that you cannot get to the Field of Challenge on time. Gamesmaster could have told you this.

Will you wait till Salim comes and tell him to let you go — 37, or try and escape — 145.

45

You draw your sword. The worm comes at you very fast. You slash at it with your sword. The sword does not go into the body. The scales stop it. You will have to try for a weak spot. (If there is one!).

The **Worm of Orbos** has 12 Fighting Skill points.

If you win — 2, if you lose — 146.

46

You go on alone. Rula and Hamid go home. This will let you make good time. You have come half-way with three days to go. Now you can go only two ways to the Castle, into the Desert — 152, or into the Swamp — 167.

47

You let her come into your mind. She does not speak but you hear her in your mind. She tells you about the Crown, the Sword and the Mace — 30.

48

You will have to get rid of the Magic in the sword. You chant a spell. "Magic go. Do not glow!" The band of blue that is the Crown of the Sun King on your head glows. The glow of the Troll's sword is no more. The Troll screams in rage. The sword now has no Magic power. Now you can attack! — 101.

49

Your sword cuts right into the Beast's neck. The Beast's head sags. The Beast slides into the water. You can go and look at the cases in the corner — 137, go and meet the others at the gate — 36, visit the old Library — 84, or go to the underground Caves — 119.

50

You take out the Sword of Prost. The Eagle is angry that you will fight it. It attacks. You turn to one side and slice its head off. The Sword has power now! The Eagle lies dead. It is a pity that you no longer have time to get to the Castle. Salim takes over the Kingdom because you are not at the Field of Challenge in time!

51

You see that he will be too quick for you. Magic is your only chance. You chant a spell, "By my will, be still!" You hold out the Mace of the Sun King. It glows blue.

The **Dark Elf** has 14 Fighting Skill points.

If you win — 158, if you lose — 43.

52

You chant a spell. The Crown glows blue. The face gets very angry. "You dare to attack me! Then face the Demon" — 83.

53

Rula has good Combat skills. This means that she is fit and strong. She also has good climbing skills from all the hunting she does. The People of the Plains often go to the Mountains to hunt. Rula climbs up the rock face. She gets the bit of the Sword of Prost. You put it with the other bits. You go to the Forge. You take Lori along. Mork flames now and then to let Lori know that she is there. You get to the Forge — 21.

54

You choose to shoot with a bow and arrow. You meet the best shot of the Elves. This will not be easy. You go down to a clear place in the woods. There are targets set on the trees. You start by shooting 10 paces away. You both hit the Bulls-eye. You then move back each time. At last you are at 100 metres! The Elf fires first. He hits the Bulls-eye in the middle! Your only hope is to shoot an arrow that splits his arrow. Can you do it?

The **Elf Archer** has 11 Fighting Skill points.

If you win — 132, if you lose — 131.

55

You feel so tired. You give up. Salim spares your life but takes over as Ruler. You have lost at the last!

56

You walk down to the Docks. The Docks are all falling into the river. There are some places standing. You go into one large warehouse. Part of the warehouse faces the river. You go over to look at some cases in the corner. Then you hear a noise from the river. You go over to take a look. A huge snake-like thing rears up from the river. It has a long body with scales. Its face has a blunt nose with fangs sticking out of a wide mouth. It has deep staring eyes. As you look into the eyes you feel weak. It is the Water Beast, a thing of some Magic. The scales are fish-like. They are covered in slime and it will not be easy to grasp. The thing seems hungry. Prepare to fight the **Water Beast.** Throw your dice and work out your Fighting Skill. Will you use Magic — 7, Weapons — 88 or Combat — 166?

57

The Troll aims at your head. You duck. The Troll's other hand comes up. It has a dagger in it! The dagger slips into your ribs. Just as it goes into your lungs you see your band of Questers die too!

Your adventure ends.

58

You cannot get near him with weapons — 127.

59

You set out to visit the Dwarves. The Dwarf King, Thon, is an old friend of yours. (See the Crown of the Sun-King). Thon is pleased to see you. You tell him of your Quest. He would like to send someone with you but has a problem. The Dwarf caves are being attacked by a huge worm. It is the Gem eating Worm of Orbos. It is eating all the Dwarves' jewels. This the Dwarves do not like. Will you help the Dwarves — 153, or go back and see where else you can go — 81?

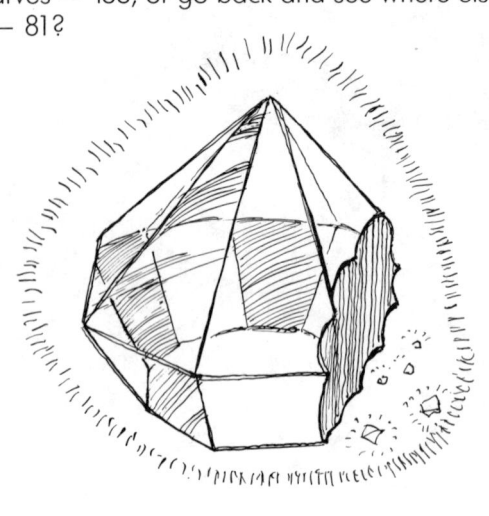

60

You will try out your new powers. The time of Challenge always has some trials for Knights the day before. You kit yourself out as the Blue Knight. You will join the trials that afternoon. First you join the Trials of Combat. The first few rounds are easy. You throw the others out of the ring. At last things are harder. In one great fight you manage to win only by a trick of dwarf fighting that Ganli showed you. Then the Final! You are up against a large man with black hair and heavy features. He looks strong. He may have some Troll blood you think. He also looks fast and fit. He has oiled his body to make it hard to grip. He is the **Combat Master.** Prepare to fight him. Throw your dice and work out your Fighting Skill — 156.

61

You agree. The Dark Elf tells you that you need a word of power to mend the Sword of Prost. When the time comes to find the forge you must say it. He tells you that the word is **'Tsorp'.** Write down this word on your list. You can also add one to your Life point score.

When you let the Dark Elf go he runs down one of the passages. You can now go and meet the others by the Gate — 36, visit the Docks — 56, or go to the old Library — 84.

62

Hamid seems to have gone into some kind of trance. He cannot help — 147.

63

Gamesmaster hears what you have to say about the trials. You have learnt a lot about how your new powers work.

You talk to Gamesmaster about the skills you will use in the Challenge. You then get an early night. You sleep well and have a good breakfast. You do some warm-ups with Gamesmaster and feel ready for the Challenge! — 149.

64

You chant a spell. You hold out your hand. You say "Turn Worm. Worm Return!" The Worm slows down. It turns round and round. Your Magic has not sent it away, but the Worm is now very slow. You can use Weapons on it — 65.

65

The Worm still has hard scales. You will have to look for a weak spot. You draw your sword.
The **Worm of Orbos** has 9 Fighting Skill points.
If you win — 2, if you lose — 146.

66

Hamid seems to be filled with power. He has gone into a kind of trance. You hear his voice in your mind. He will show you what to do. The Elven Forge speaks to him as he is an Elf. You then tell the others of their tasks. Hamid shows you.

Rula takes the bits of the Sword out of your pack. Do you have the **Magic Metal** (check your Equipment List)?
If you have the Magic Metal — 67. If you do not have it — 3.

67

You take out the Magic Metal mould. Rula places the bits of Sword inside. Ganli puts some of the ore from Death Mountain into the mould. Rula also puts the hilt of the Sword in its place in the mould.

Then you call Mork over. Mork flames at the mould. Dragon fire heats the molten metal. The metal glows yellow, then white and blue. Mork lifts out the mould with her claws. (Dragon skin cannot be burnt by fire.) She plunges the mould into the pool of water. A loud hiss is heard. Clouds of steam rise up. Ganli wraps a bit of leather around his hand. He takes the Sword hilt. He holds the Sword blade on to the flat rock. He pounds the Sword with a silver hammer. (All Dwarves carry hammers in case they find gold or jewels in rocks!)

Mork flames at the blade to keep it soft. Then you point to Lori. Lori frowns, but still raises his hands. Green light comes from his hands. The light flows into the blade. You keep pointing at Lori until he falls to the ground. He is very tired. All the while you feel Hamid in your mind. He puts his own magic into the Sword. He makes sure all goes as it should.

At last all is done. Ganli puts a sharp edge to the Sword. A last dip into the pool of water ends it all. You all place a hand (or a claw!) on the cool blade. All chant:

"Human lifted,
Dragon fired,
Magi spelled,
Dwarf beaten
Elf guided
Sword moulded"

The Sword of Prost glows with a light like blue fire. The band of Questers give you the Sword. You are the Ruler of the Secret Land. You take the Sword. The Sword, Mace and Crown all light up with the same blue light.

You feel great power flow into you. Add 5 to your Life point score.

Now you are ready to meet the Challenge of Salim — 124.

68

You take no notice. The yellow shape gets close. It opens it's mouth. You are a little upset — 106.

69

The Captain is so fast that he has the dagger at your throat before you can lift your Sword. The people now see who you are. They do not want a ruler that can be beaten in the trials. You have lost.

70

Hamid cannot reach Lori. Also his Magic is not the kind to help here — 142.

71

The Black Dragon laughs at your silly games. A huge claw slams into you. You are thrown to the ground. The Dragon flames you to ash!

Your adventure is over!

72

Just as you feel that the Magi are too strong the ball leaps up. It shoots up to the top of the hall. The force is so great that it breaks the roof. The ball can be seen rising into the sky. The Magi all look at you. Bori says, "You have done well!" The Magi all clap. You have beaten them all. (You can't help thinking that it was all too easy!) One of the Magi, Lori, will go with you on your Quest. Add **Lori** to your List of Questers on your adventure sheet.

You now go back to the Castle and choose where to go next — 81.

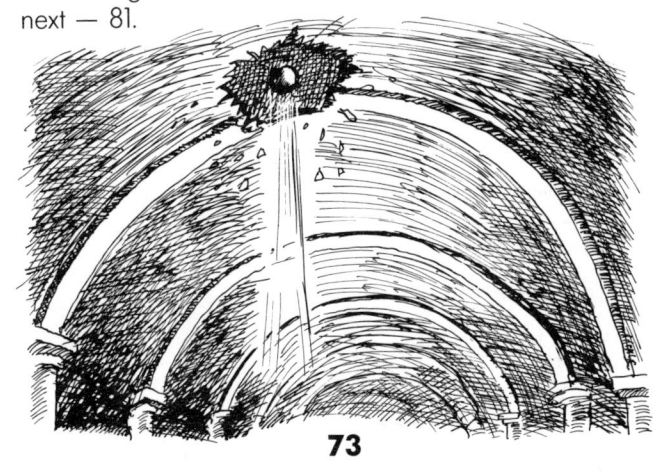

73

You are wrong again! The band of Questers are very upset. They do not like all these things you are saying about them. They all get fed up and leave you. You cannot finish your Quest unless all are present. Your Quest fails!

74

You take out the Magic Ore from Death Mountain. The face says, "That is Magic Ore from Death Mountain". Nothing else happens. Go back to 39 and try again.

75

You draw your sword. The bear looks very angry. It is about to charge you. It is a pity that you are going to try and kill him. After all you did wake him up. If you still want to fight him go to 18, or you can try Magic — 28, or Combat — 136.

76

You take out your sword. This is not a magic sword of course. The warrior takes out her own sword. The red fire gleams off the blade. She twists and turns the blade. She looks as if she has fine skills in sword fighting. This is because she is the best warrior of the tribe. This was not a good idea!

The **Warrior Woman** has 14 Fighting Skill points.

If you win — 160. If you lose — 144.

77

You wait for Rula and Hamid to get back their strength. On Day 4 you set off again. You only have 2 days to travel 3 days' distance at the pace you can go. You are too late. Salim takes over the Kingdom as there is no one at the Field of Challenge.

You have failed!

78

You step to one side. The Troll charges past. You put your foot out and he crashes to the ground. Quick as a flash you place your boot on his chest. Your sword point is at his throat. The Troll looks up at you. He gives up his sword. Add one to your Life point score.

The Troll agrees to let you have some of the **Magic Ore** (write it on your Equipment List). Ganli, the Dwarf, helps to mine the ore. As you leave Death Mountain you think again about the trap. Who can have told the Trolls to be where they were?

Now that you have the ore you will have to find the old Elven Forge. Nobody, not even the Elves, know where it is. Hamid, the Elf, says that you may find something to help in the old Elf city. The old city, Elvon, now lies in bits of brick and plaster. It can be found past the desert and to the West. You all set out for Elvon. Go to 103.

79

You get ready for your quest. You pack food and take the three bits of the Sword of Prost with you. You also take a non-magic sword with you to fight with — 81.

80

You jump away from the path. That was rather foolish. The path was not wide. You fall off the path. Lose 2 Life Points. You fall into the air. You see the yellow shape rush at you. You are lifted up back to the path — 106.

81

Where will you start your Quest?

You can:
Go to the Mountains — 164
Visit the Dragons — 13
Visit the Men of the Plains — 150
Visit the Dwarves — 59
Visit the Elves — 95
Visit the Magi — 120.

82

You have done so well that the Elf Queen grants help to your Quest. The Elf that you were sent against goes with you. The Elf's name is Hamid. Write **Hamid** on your list of Questers. He is tall and fair. Before you go the Queen tells you a tale of the Sword of Prost.

The Queen tells you that all the races of the Secret Land are needed to mend the Sword. All the races must help for the full power of the Sword to come. The Queen also tells you that the Sword was made from ore from Death Mountain. When the Elves used the Elven forge they used this ore. The ore from Death Mountain must be used again to mend the Sword. You will have to go and get some of this ore.

Do you have all the races with you (Mork the Dragon, Rula the Woman, Ganli the Dwarf, Lori the Magi and Hamid the Elf?). If you do you may go on to 165. If you do not have all the races go to 81.

83

The air in front of you glows. It feels hot. Out of the air you see a red shape. It looks a bit like an Elf, but has red skin. Its eyes are also red and fire comes from its fingers. It has hairy legs with hooves as feet. This is not going to be an easy thing to get by. Will you use Magic — 11, Weapons — 141, or Combat — 32.

84

You go into a building. You see rows of books. Most of them have rotted away. Some of them are still in one piece. You come to a dark part of the Library. You are just about to go out when you hear a noise. You turn and see a shape standing there. It is an old elf. He has a long beard and a wise look on his face. He does not seem real. Is it a dream? As you stand there you feel a cold feeling creep over your body. It seems as if ice is inside you. The old elf looks at you with an evil eye. It is the **Elf Wraith**. Prepare to fight him. Throw your dice and work out your Fighting Skill — 98.

85

You look at Ganli. He is small. He could have been the figure that you saw in the desert. But why would he warn you of the Trolls only to get them to ambush you later? Also, he does not have any Magic to use the message globe. You are wrong. If this is your first guess go to 17 and try again. If this is not your first guess — 73.

86

Lori laughs when he sees that you will try to beat his Magic. You try to say a spell but you cannot. You cannot open your mouth. Lori lifts up his hands. A green light of Magic power hits you. You find that you have been moved to a grey misty place. You will be lost here forever. Your Quest has failed.

87

You take out your sword. The Troll aims a blow. You block it with your sword. Red sparks fly about. You feel a pain in your arm. Lose 4 Life points! The Magic in the Troll's sword is strong. You will have to get rid of it. Will you use Combat — 128 or Magic — 48.

88

You take out your sword. The beast tries to look at you with its eyes. You do not look into its eyes. You look at its mouth. The beast has slime all over it. The skin is soft. The scales are not hard. Your sword will cut it easily. You slash at the beast's neck as it comes at you.

The **Water Beast** has 15 Fighting Skill points.

If you win — 49, if you lose — 114.

89

You run on. High above you hear the harsh cry of an Eagle. You think about the very start of your adventures. You think how an Eagle's cry started you out to find Grom (in the Castle of Grom adventure). Can the Eagle help you now? If you will stop to call to the Eagle for help — 35. If you will run on — 130.

90

Dragons also have some Magic. Lose 2 Life points and then choose Combat — 41 or Weapons — 102.

91

You draw your sword across his throat. The Dark Elf dies. You feel a little ashamed. You wonder whether his secret was important. You can now visit the Docks — 56, the old Library — 84 or go and meet the others by the Gate — 36.

92

The next day you set off to find the Elven Forge. You look at the map. A bit of the map is missing! All of the map was there when you first got it. Sometime, after you met the others, a bit of the map has been taken.

The bit that is gone showed the place where the Elven Forge is. The map shows that the Forge is in the Land of Volcanoes, but not the place where the Forge can be found. Someone does not want you to mend the Sword of Prost. None of the others say that they know anything about the map. You set off to go to the Land of Volcanoes. This is where the Fell Lord used to live. (You beat him in the Crown of the Sun-King adventure.) You will need to find the lava mountain where the Forge is.

After a time of travel you come to the mountains. As the last bit of the map is missing you do not know where to go. Will you go up the mountain path — 148 or into a cave in the side of the mountain — 123.

93

In a month, Salim comes for the Challenge. Salim's magic and his sword are too strong for you. You have no Sword. He beats you and takes over the Secret Land. You are sent away! Your adventure ends here! — Start again.

94

Your only chance is to try Weapons — 88, or Magic — 7.

95

You set off for the woods. The Elves live in the woods in gold and silver trees. You take the path that the Elf men took you on last time. (In the Castle of Grom adventure.)

At last you meet the Elf Queen again. She is still very fair, but stern. You tell her of your Quest. She says that she will help if you can do well at an Elf sport. You can choose to compete against the **Elf Runner** — 116, or the **Elf Archer** with a bow and arrow — 168.

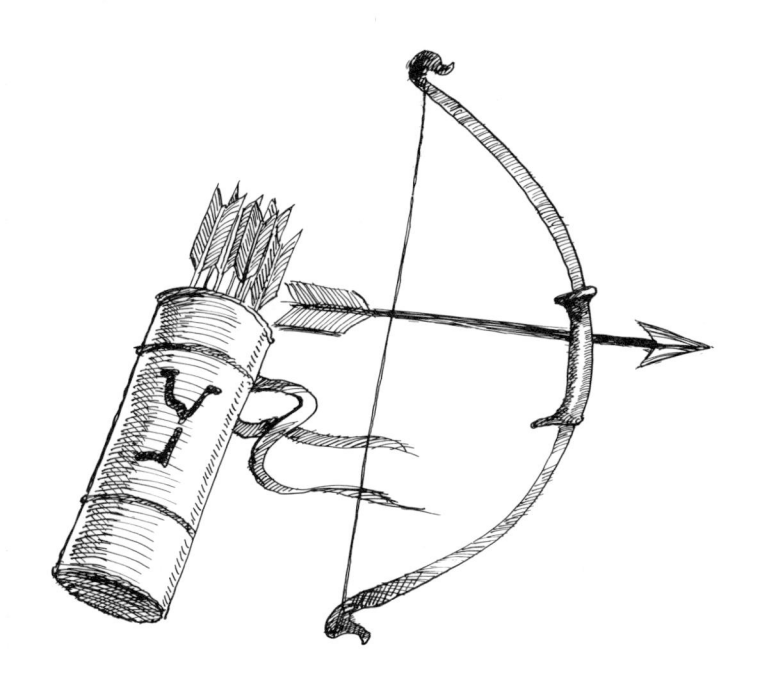

96

You look at Hamid. He would know something about the Elven Forge and maybe the Elves do not want it found again. He would also have some Magic for the message globe. Yet, he looks a bit large for the figure you saw in the desert. He also told you about the Demon guard. He could have been quiet then. You are wrong. If this is your first guess go to 17 and try again. If this is not your first guess — 73.

97

The Weapon trials are full of hopeful soldiers. You do not hurt any too badly in the early rounds. The Final puts you up against a Captain of the Guard. He is well known for his skill. He sees who you are at once. You wink at him and he says nothing. The Captain's weapons are Dagger and Short Sword. These are very fast and quick. You have to be careful of attack from both sides. You both bow. Then he moves forward with the speed of a snake. You jump to one side and feel a Dagger slash past you. The trials are to first blood, not to death.

The **Weapon Master** has 25 Fighting Skill points.

If you lose — 69. If you win — 40.

98

You feel yourself getting colder and colder. You will freeze to death unless you do something. Combat and Weapons will be useless against this ghost-like being. You will have to use Magic. You lift your hand and say a spell, "Like the morn, let it be warm!" You feel a little bit of heat. The Crown begins to glow.

The **Elf Wraith** has 14 Fighting Skill points.

If you win — 5, if you lose — 107.

99

You take up a stance for Combat. The Dark Elf laughs. He does not put his sword away. He has no sense of fair play! He just comes at you with his sword. Will you be able to beat a being so well trained? He is so fast, and he has a sword. Try Weapons — 115.

100

The ball crashes to the ground. The Magi have won. Your Quest is over.

101

You now fight the Troll sword to sword. You will have to use your skill. The Troll has strength but is slow. You wave your sword in front of his eyes. You dance round him. The Troll puts his head down and charges!

The **Troll King** has 15 Fighting Skill points.

If you win — 78, if you lose — 57.

102

Oh dear! You did not learn much from your fight with Bork. (In the Crown of the Sun-King adventure.) Dragons have very hard skin. You also do not have a Magic Sword. This is going to be a hard fight for you. You take out your sword. The Dragon flames at you.

The **Black Dragon** has 13 Fighting Skill points.

If you lose — 71, if you win — 23.

103

You need to walk across the Desert to get to Elvon. That night you camp in the Desert. After the heat of the day it gets very cold. You cannot sleep. Late in the night you go for a walk to keep warm. You see a glow coming from behind a rock. When you walk round the rock you see a small figure. It has a glass globe in its hand. You can see figures moving in the globe. Is it some kind of signal? Just as you go to ask what is going on the figure sees you. It quickly runs off. When you get back to the camp all the band of Questers seem to be asleep. You think that one of them must be awake. None answer when you call. After a short time you go back to sleep. The next morning you say nothing. You head west to Elvon — 110.

104

You take out the Mace. It glows blue. The power of the Mace lets you talk to the Eagle. You tell it how you must get to the Castle soon. The Eagle is a huge giant Eagle. It is the same one that gave you the Crown of the Dragon King. He bends forward. You see a saddle and straps! You climb up. As you fly off you wonder just what this Eagle is. Then, in an hour or two, you see the Castle. You have arrived on the afternoon of Day 5!

You can go and find Gamesmaster and ask him what has been going on — 157 or you can go and find Salim at once — 44.

105

You say that you will try the task of the Magi. Bori leads you to a great hall. The room has seven sides. All around sit Magi. They are the rulers and the best Magic users of Rangorn. In the centre of the hall is a ball of light. It floats in mid air and is like a green fog. Your task, Bori tells you, is to make the ball rise up in the air. The Magi will try to stop you with their Magic.

The Magi all close their eyes. They chant all at once. A low sound can be heard. The ball sinks to the ground. You lift your hand and say "Ball rise, up to the Skies." You then raise your pointed hand. The ball follows. The Magi chant. The ball sinks. You are locked in Magic with the Magi. The ball goes up and down. You feel your Magic power at full strength.

The **Magi Elders** have 9 Fighting Skill Points.

If you win — 72 if you lose — 100.

106

The yellow shape was Mork. She laughs and laughs to see the fright she gave you. She has been flying round and round while you plod up the mountain. You walk on. You make some comments about how foolish dragons are. Mork pretends not to hear. She says that the path goes into the mountain at the top.

You come to the end of the path. The path goes into the black rock. You see some steps cut into the rock there. At the top of the steps is a black shape. It is shiny and is like a face carved into the rock. As you get closer the face speaks, "Who dares enter the Mount of Elves!" It is some kind of Guard. You can tell Hamid, the Elf to come forward — 26, or walk on past the face — 163.

107

The heat from your Magic is too little for the cold of the Elf. The Crown stops glowing. It gets colder and colder until you are a block of ice. Your heart stops! The Elf still smiles! Your adventure is over.

108

You use the word of power. You shout **"Tsorp"** in a firm voice. The face says, "You have the password to the Elven Forge. You and your band may go in." The Demon fades away. It was not real, just an Elf trick — 16.

109

The violet ropes come towards you. Quickly you chant a spell to awake the Mace. It glows blue and all the ropes blow away. You then find that you are drawn into those violet eyes! They are making you sleepy. You cast a spell to awake the Crown. The Magic Mistress is no match for the Crown. You wake and send a dream to her. She will awake in ten minutes or so. The crowd cheers again. More are looking at you as if they know you. They follow you as you go to the Weapon trials. This is your final trial. You must prepare to fight the **Weapon Master.** Throw your dice and work out your Fighting Skill — 97.

110

At last you come to the old city of Elvon. It has fallen over the years but is still very fair. Some tall thin towers are still standing. There are also domes covered in tiles of many colours. Huge walls still stand. The gates have long since rotted away. The city was built on a river that goes into the sea nearby. The river still runs to the sea on the West. To the East is the Desert. This was once good land. The Elves moved when it became Desert many hundreds of years ago. You all go into the city. When you get inside you all go to look at parts of the city. You agree to meet at the old gates at the end of the day. You can visit the Docks — 56, the old Library — 84, the underground Caves — 119, or go to the Gate to meet the others — 36.

111

You try to cast a spell. You say "Mind out, turn about". Her mind has great power. You can do nothing. She does not speak but you hear her in your mind. She tells you about the Crown, the Sword and the Mace — 30.

112

Ganli is too short to reach Lori. He also has no Magic — 142.

113

You set off at a fast jog with Hamid and Rula. The rest of the Questers go back to their homes. Lori says that the Magi will get their own back for what you did. The others promise friendship.

You can go at this pace—walk, jog, run, walk, for a long time. After two days you have gone one third of the way to the Castle. On the third day Rula and Hamid are very tired. You have the strength of the Mace, Sword and Crown to help you. You can go on alone — 46, or wait for a day to give them some rest — 77.

114

The head of the Beast sways to one side. Your sword goes past its neck. The Beast eats you up. Your adventure ends!

115

You draw your sword. It is a pity it is not a magic sword. The Dark Elf that you will fight has a magic sword. He is also a very skilled swordsman.

The **Dark Elf** has 19 Fighting Skill points.

If you win — 25. If you lose — 135.

116

You say that you will run a race. You will run with the fastest Elf. You will be running 5 miles! This looks like it will be a long race. You both set off. There is a line of Elves on each side of the trees. Some cheer for you and others cheer for the Elf. The Elf runs very fast over the first mile. You are way behind him. He darts past trees and over streams. After 3 miles you are tired — 143.

117

Ganli tries. He just cannot reach the first hand hold. He will not help you here — 31.

118

You fall asleep. You do not wake up again. The Beast has eaten you! Your adventure is over!

119

You see some steps that go down into the ground. You take them. After a time you come to a passage. You walk along for about a mile. Then you come to some underground caves. You hear a noise from one of them. You go into it. there are more passages going off this cave. Just in the passages is a tall being. At first you think it is an Elf. It has the same pointed ears. Then you see that it has black hair and not fair hair. Also its skin is a dead white. The being looks at you. It has a mean looking mouth. It sneers and draws it's sword. It looks very strong and has the body of one trained to fight. It swishes the sword about with great speed. The sword glows a little. It is the **Dark Elf.** You will have to fight. Throw your dice and work out your Fighting Skill. Will you use Weapons — 115, Magic — 51 or Combat — 99?

120

You take the long road to the Magi. The Magi are Magic users of great skill. They are known for being clever. They are very small beings, with long odd ears. The Magi live by the sea in a walled city. No one can go into the city unless the Magi allow it. The city is called Rangorn.

When you get to Rangorn the Magi let you in. You are, after all, their Ruler. They also let any that are with you come in. You are given a meal and a bath. Then you meet Bori, the Head of the Magi. Bori has a tall hat on his head. He looks at you out of the side of his eyes. After you tell your tale he looks sly. He then asks you if you will fight the Magi Elders with Magic as a test. If you will you must prepare to fight the **Magi Elders.** Throw your dice and work out your fighting skill points — 105. If you will not fight, you return to the Castle — 81.

121

What! Combat on a 20 metre long worm? You strike the Worm with a punch. It takes no notice. You try a flying kick. The Worm takes no notice. You leap on its back. It rolls over and crushes you. Lose 4 Life points. You must try Weapons — 45 or Magic — 64.

122

You and Salim both take a lance. You charge towards each other on your horses. The lances meet together in a great crash! Both the lances break. You take new lances. You turn and charge again. Both strike true! You fall to the ground, as does Salim. You try to get your breath back. Just then you feel a blast of power that slams you to the ground. Salim has sent a bolt of Magic power from a jewel set in his helmet. You feel so tired. You throw off the feeling and get to your feet.

You then both draw your Sword. The Sword of Prost glows with power. Your blows send Salim reeling backwards. The Sword of Prost crashes again and again into Salim. Then Salim twists his foot to one side. He trips you up. Salim's fist crashes into your nose. You lie there stunned. Salim lifts up his sword and places it against your throat.

Salim has 40 Fighting Skill points.

If you win — 169, if you lose — 55.

123

You go into a cave in the side of the mountain. There does not seem to be any way out. The cave is a dead-end. You think that there is nothing in here at first. You turn to go out. Then you hear a roar. It is a bear. The bear has been sleeping in the cave. It is not happy that you came in. It has been woken up and is angry! It stands on its back legs. It is huge! It has large claws and must be about 150 kilos! Will you use Weapons — 75, Combat — 136, or Magic — 28.

124

You do not have much time left to get back to the Castle. If you are not there when Salim goes onto the Challenge Field you will lose. You must get to the Castle in six days. This is Day One. Will you ask Mork to fly you to the Castle — 9, or will you take Rula and Hamid with you and march — 113.

125

You take out your Staff. It is long, heavy wood. The pole-like weapon can crack open a shin or a skull when used in skilled hands. The woman also takes out a Staff. She makes the Staff sing in the air as it goes round and round. You see that she is a little unsure how to use it. She has training but has not used the Staff as much as you. The Staff was a weapon that you used many times with Gamesmaster at the Castle. A good weapon!

The **Warrior Woman** has 10 Fighting Skill Points.

If you lose — 144, if you win — 160.

126

You look at Rula. The people of the Plains are proud. Maybe they do not want to have a Ruler. Rula may have been kneeling when you saw the figure in the Desert. Yet, you do not think the figure was a woman. You also recall just how close Rula was to beating you in the fight you had. If she had won that fight she would not be on the Quest. Also she has no Magic for the message globe. You are wrong. If this is your first guess go to 17 and try again. If this is not your first guess — 73.

127

You try to attack. Lori laughs when he sees you run at him. He rises off the ground. You have made a mistake. You try to fight him with your Magic. You know the Magi are the best Magic users in the land, but it is your only hope. You will not be able to get near him with Combat or Weapons. Go to — 154.

128

You rush at the Troll King and use a fist strike. The Troll takes the blow on his chest and laughs. "You will have to do better than that!" He roars. A great blow from his fist sends you to the ground. He stands over you, fists ready!

The **Troll King** has 19 Fighting Skill points.

If you win — 140. If you lose — 57.

129

You try to grip him, but cannot. Your best punches and kicks are shrugged off. He then knocks you out of the ring. The people then see who you are. They will not take a Ruler that can be beaten in a Trial. Salim has won!

130

You take no more notice of the Eagle. You run, jog, run, for miles. After the next day you come to the Castle. It is Day 6. It is 10 a.m. Salim is just going into the Field of Challenge. You are just in time. You run on to the Field of Challenge to meet Salim. You are tired. You have had no time to try out your new Sword. Lose 5 Life points — 161.

131

Slowly you pull back the bow. The watching crowd holds its breath. You take note of the wind. You let fly! The arrow just misses the Elf's arrow. You have lost! The Queen is still surprised at your shooting — 82.

132

Slowly you pull the bow back. The watching crowd holds its breath. You take note of the wind. You let fly! The arrow strikes the Elf's arrow. It splits it neatly. You have won. The Queen is very surprised at your shooting — 82.

133

The Eagle sees that you are about to use a spell. You hold out your hand and chant "Eagle . . .". The rest of your spell is stopped short. The Eagle's beak has slashed your arm, try Weapons — 22 or Combat — 50.

134

Lori sneers at you. He changes from a sweet little old man to a nasty rat-like man! "Yes, you fool" he snarls, "Do you think you could beat the might of the Magi! I also took the bit of map when you let me see the Magic Metal. Now die you worm!" Lori gets ready to put a Magic spell on you. Will you use Magic — 15, Combat — 127 or Weapons — 58?

135

The Dark Elf is very quick. He turns and twists to one side. The blows you aim at him go by. He mocks you with an evil smile. You attack with great force. It is no good. The Dark Elf is too quick! You feel his sword jab into your heart. That is the last thing you feel! Your adventure is over.

136

You are going to fight a bear that is angry with your bare hands! This is very foolish. You punch the bear's belly. It roars again and folds you in it's arms. Bear hugs are not called bear hugs for nothing. Lose 4 Life points. Use Weapons — 75, or Magic — 28.

137

You go over to the corner of the room. There you see many cases. One of them has a mark on it. The mark is shaped like a sword. You open the case. Inside is a solid metal rectangle. It is very long with the shape of a sword in it. It is a mould used to make a sword. Molten steel or iron can be poured into it. It is a metal mould that was used by the Elves to make Swords of power. You try to pick it up. To your surprise it is very light! The metal has Magic in it. This will help you forge the Sword of Prost. You take it with you. (Write the **Magic Metal** down on your Equipment List.) Now you may go to the Gate to meet the others — 36, the underground Cave — 119 or the old Library — 84.

138

Your Magic, without your full power, is weak. It can still make Lori's spells miss even if you cannot beat him. The green light has hit your pack. You see a flash of light. One of the bits of the Sword of Prost flies into the air. It goes into Lori's hand. You cannot forge a new Sword without all the bits! Lori laughs. "Your quest must fail!" He starts a spell to take him back to the city of the Magi. What can you do to stop him? He begins to rise up higher and higher into the air. Who will you ask to help you? — 142.

139

You say that as Ruler of the Secret Land you will rid the Dragons of this mad thing. You take the road out to the desert. The Black Dragon has been seen there last. You have not gone far when you hear a roar. It is the fire of the Black Dragon. He flies over you like a huge black cloud. As he flies by, a jet of red hot flame shoots at you. You hold up the Mace. A blue light shines out and the fire crashes onto the light. The Mace is like a shield. The Black Dragon flies by again. It is angry now and its red eyes look down at you. The hard skin of the Dragon shines a deep black. You can run away — 81, or prepare to fight the **Black Dragon.** Remember to throw your dice and work out your Fighting Skill. Will you use Magic — 90, use Combat — 41 or use Weapons — 102?

140

You duck under his long arms. You let him come at you. Then you throw him over. The Troll crashes into the wall. He is still strong. You will have to finish this with your sword — 78.

141

You take out your sword. You slash at the Demon. Its hands turn the sword to one side. Your sword does not cut its hand. Nothing you do seems to harm it. You can try Magic — 11, Combat — 32, or ask the others to help — 151.

142

You can choose one of these:—

Rula — (human, female, no Magic but good at Combat, Weapons and Hunting) — 10. Ganli — (dwarf, male, no Magic, but good at Weapons. Very fierce and can go fighting mad with his Axe) — 112. Mork — (dragon, female, has Magic and some Combat. Seems fierce but is very kind really) — 29. Hamid — (elf, male, has Magic of the mind, and some Combat and Weapon skills) — 70.

143

You see that the Elf is also tired. This makes you feel better. You run faster. Slowly you seem to be catching up. Can you catch up before the end of the race? — 6.

144

The woman is fast and strong. She slashes your leg and wins the fight. Your Quest fails! Your adventure is over.

145

The men go. They put the Sword of Prost by the tent wall. They leave the Crown and Mace. You close your eyes. Slowly you feel the power light up the Crown. Very slowly you try to stretch your ropes.

All this takes time. By the time you get free it is the next morning. You grab your sword. You rush out. You see Salim on the Field of Challenge. You are tired and have had no time to try out the Sword of Prost. Lose 5 Life points — 161.

146

You thrust your sword between the Worm's scales. Thin green blood comes out. The worm does not seem to notice. Its vast mouth opens out. You thrust your sword into the soft back of the throat. The Worm grinds you up with its teeth. You die as Worm food!

147

Ganli — 12. Hamid — 62.

148

You go up the side of the mountain. The path is steep. It is only a few feet wide. Soon you are very high up the mountain. The rocks are dark. Far below you see where you have come from. You are all walking one behind the other now. Just as you near the top of the mountain you see a huge shape come out of the sky at you. It is yellow. Will you draw your sword — 4, take no notice — 68, or jump away from the path — 80.

149

You dress in Blue Armour. You take a grey horse and go to the Field of Challenge. A fanfare of trumpets sound. Salim enters the Field. He wears black armour, and rides a white horse. The trumpets sound again. You race onto the Field and lift your helmet. Salim's eyes go wide with shock as he sees you. The prizes from the Trials can be seen on your sleeve. This will be a long hard fight. Prepare to fight Salim. Throw your dice and work out your Fighting Skill. You feel good. You have tried out your power and are ready for him. You can add 3 to your fighting skill. That gives you a fighting skill of 37 on your Adventure Sheet — 122.

150

You go to the Plains. The Plains are a stretch of land that forms grassland past the desert. The Men of the Plains hunt buffalo and other animals there. They are a very proud race. They are also skilled at hunting and tracking.

You find the camp of the People of the Plains. There you meet the Chief. He asks you to stay for a meal. Around the campfire you tell the Chief of your Quest. As the Chief thinks about what you say a young woman sits close to you. You ask her to get you some more drink. The woman jumps up in a rage. You are not thinking well! The woman is the best warrior and hunter in the tribe. You have made a mistake by thinking her a campfire help! The warrior asks the Chief for your head! The Chief thinks this is a great joke. He tells you that he will send someone to aid your Quest if you can beat the warrior in a fight. This must be a fight using Weapons. This will make it a fair fight. The warrior wants a fight to the death. The Chief says that it will be to first blood only. Prepare to fight the **Warrior Woman.** Throw your dice and work out your Fighting Skill.

The warrior wanted to fight. This means that you can take the weapon you want. You can take the Sword — 76, the Hunting Knife — 162, or the Staff — 125.

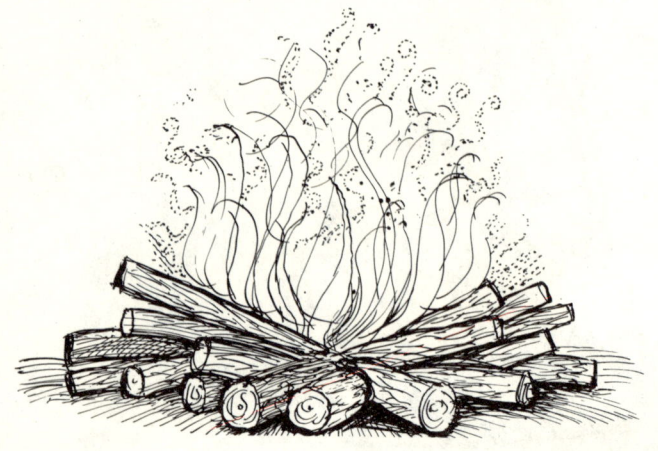

151

You ask the others to help. Mork flames at the Demon but just gets a hot backlash. Rula and Ganli have no more luck than you. The Demon still stares. Lori just shrugs and says he can do nothing. Hamid says that Elves do not like to harm people and that this must be to scare people off. There must be some strong spell to stop anyone going past. The Demon is not real. The spell works by turning back any attack onto itself. As your Magic cannot get past the spell, you check your Equipment List for anything that might help — 39.

152

You choose the Desert. The Desert is hot by day and cold by night. You do not make good time. You leave the Desert. You are now on Day 5 — 89.

153

You tell the Dwarf King that you will help with the Worm. He tells you that the Worm was last seen in the East passage. You walk down that way. It is very dark. You cannot see anything, but there is a smell of something rotten. You go round a corner. It is light here from torches on the wall. Then you see it. The Worm is huge, with a green body. It is 20 metres long. Its body is as thick as a horse. It has hard scales. The Worm is covered in slime and stinks. The Worm has no eyes but uses smell to find its prey. It has rows and rows of grinding teeth. These are to grind up the gems. These teeth are now coming for you! Prepare to fight the **Worm of Orbos.** Throw your dice and work out your Fighting Skill. Will you use Combat — 121, Weapons — 45 or Magic — 64?

154

Lori laughs when he sees you try to beat his Magic. Lori lifts his hands. A green light of Magic power hits you. You say a spell, "Magic hide, to one side!". Lori's Magic is moved and now the green light hits your pack — 138.

155

You look at Mork. You see a large Dragon. Could she have been the little figure you saw with the globe in the desert? You are wrong. Go to 17 and try again.

156

The **Combat Master** has 19 Fighting Skill points.

If you lose — 129, if you win — 27.

157

You go to find Gamesmaster. He tells you that Salim knows you are away. Salim has told all his men to keep a look out for you. If they find you they are to grab you. You will be tied up and cannot get to the Field of Challenge on time. Gamesmaster advises that you try out your new powers. Then you can rest and meet Salim in the morning. Will you go and see Salim now — 44, or do what the Gamesmaster advises — 60.

158

The Dark Elf smiles in an evil way. His sword lights up red. He has some Magic too. Your Magic is stronger. Soon his sword is just a lump of iron. The Dark Elf gets slower and slower. Soon he cannot move. Your spell has made him still. You take out your sword and place it at his throat. You then let your Magic fall from him — 38.

159

Elves are not very good climbers of rocks. They are all right with trees, but tend to stay in woodland. Hamid cannot help here — 31.

160

You dance round one another in the firelight. The woman is light on her feet. She is fast and strong. Your weapons clash again and again. You turn back and feel the air on your face as the weapon rushes by. She picks up some dust and throws it at your eyes. She hopes to blind you while she closes in. You are wise to this trick. You hold your eyes as if you are blinded, but you look out. The warrior thinks that her trick has worked. She strikes out at you. You duck and turn. As she goes by you crack your weapon sharply against her leg. A line of blood appears. The Chief calls a halt to the fight. You have won. Add one to your Life point score.

The warrior looks at you. She grins and shakes hands. She is not angry at being beaten in a fair fight. She tells you that you did well. She says that her name is Rula. She asks the Chief if she may go with you on the Quest. She will be useful as a tracker and fighter. Write **Rula** on your list of Questers.

The next day you set out with Rula. Add two to your Life point score. How many Questers do you have? If you have Mork the Dragon, Hamid the Elf, Ganli the Dwarf, Lori the Magi and Rula the Woman — 165. If you do not have all these Questers — 81 and choose where to go next.

161

This is bad news. You are tired and not ready to fight. You are dirty and it takes a long while for the people to see who you are. Salim comes up with a fanfare of trumpets. He is dressed in Black shiny armour. He rides a white horse. He sneers at you. "Is this the Ruler of the Secret Land! You do not deserve to win". He waves a hand and a horse is given to you.

The Challenge is a fight until one person gives up. Weapons, Magic and Combat can be used. Salim looks at you. He thinks he will make the fight a long one as you are tired. Prepare to fight **Salim**. Throw your dice and work out your Fighting Skill — 122.

162

You take out your knife. The warrior takes out her own knife. It is a sharp and long hunting knife. The red fire gleams off the blade. She twists and turns the blade. She looks as if she has fine skills in knife fighting. This is because she is the best hunter in the tribe. This was not a good idea!

The **Warrior Woman** has 14 Fighting Skill points.

If you win — 160. If you lose — 144.

163

You try to walk past the face. You cannot walk past. The air becomes like glue. The more you try to push past the harder it is. The face says, "To enter the Elven Forge you must pass me or fight my Demon." You will have to fight the Demon — 83.

164

Do you have all the five Questers with you? You should have Mork the Dragon, Rula the Woman, Hamid the Elf, Ganli the Dwarf and Lori the Magi. If you have all five go to 165. If you do not you must go back to the Castle and look — 81. You need all of them in your Quest.

165

You take the road to the Mountains. You tell the band of the story told you by the Elf Queen. You will go to Death Mountain to look for the ore. This will be needed to mend the Sword of Prost. Ganli does not look happy about this. That night, at camp, he tells you all that the Trolls have taken over Death Mountain. They now mine the ore for their own weapons. They say that it is their mine. They prove this by force of arms. The Troll King keeps a small army here.

You all agree on a plan. You will creep in by a secret entrance under the mine. You sleep. The next day you all set off for the secret entrance — 8.

166

You take up a stand for Combat. You try to grab the beast. It has slime all over it. You cannot get a grip. You try to punch, but this does not harm it. Trying Combat on a long, snake-like beast that you cannot hold was not a good idea! Lose 2 Life points — 94.

167

You choose the Swamp. The Swamp is trackless. You find your way but do not make good time. You leave the Swamp. You are now on Day 5 — 89.

168

Prepare to fight the **Elf Archer.** Throw your dice and work out your fighting skill — 54.

169

You feel so tired. You take power from the Crown. A blue light blinds Salim. You leap up and then it is Salim's turn to have a sword at his throat! He gives up at once. He only likes to fight every year and does not want to be killed. You spare him. You raise your sword. The crowd cheer and cheer. You are now the true Ruler with all three powers. You are unbeatable!

Late into that evening you feast. Even Salim, who is not such a bad person after all, comes along. Everyone rejoices that they have such a strong and good Ruler but you are very tired. Your Quest has been a long and difficult task. Even later that night you go to bed. You are happy. You have lived through many adventures and seen much danger. You have travelled far and learned a lot. You will be a wise and just Ruler. Now you must sleep. You close your eyes and dream. For some reason you dream of a woman with sea-green eyes.

THE SWORD OF PROST ADVENTURE SHEET

Name: ....

Each time you fight you must work out your Fighting Skill Points.

| You have already been given some Fighting Skill Points for each fight | + | Throw both your dice and write down the total number you have thrown. | = | Add these numbers together to find your Fighting Skill Points. |

Skill Points given + Dice Throw = Your Fighting Skill Points

You win if you have the same or more Fighting Skill Points than the Creature.
You lose if you have less Fighting Skill Points than the Creature.

QUESTERS

___ ___ ___ ___ ___

Life Points	Equipment List	Story Number
25		

Creature	Skill Points	Dice Throw	Your Fighting Skill Points	Creatures Fighting Skill Points	Win/Lose
Magi Elders	4	+	=		
Worm of Orbos	6	+	=		
Elf Archer	5	+	=		
Black Dragon	6	+	=		
Warrior Woman	7	+	=		
Troll King	11	+	=		
Water Beast	6	+	=		
Elf Wraith	8	+	=		
Dark Elf	9	+	=		
Combat Master	15	+	=		
Magic Mistress	16	+	=		
Weapon Master	20	+	=		
Salim	34	+	=		